MARTIN LUTHER

AND THE

REFORMATION

By

Gerald B. Winrod

Editor of The Defender.

●

THIRD PRINTING

Price 25 cents
Five Copies $1.00
One Hundred Copies $15.00

"The just shall live by faith."

Gerald B. Winrod

The above picture was taken in front of the door of historic Castle Church in Wittenberg on which Martin Luther nailed his ninety-five Theses.

THE BIRTHDAY

"BUT whom say ye that I am?"

This was the great question that Jesus put to His Church. There were only twelve members in the congregation at that time. Repeated references are made in the four Gospels to "the twelve".

It seems that soon after the Baptist baptized Jesus at Jordan's ford, a large number of people anxiously followed Him. These followers were composed of plain people. They came from the common walks of life.

As the time approached to select the pillars upon which the structure of the Church was to be built, Jesus concerned Himself with the task of selecting twelve men who could be counted on to work with Him in making the principles and doctrines of His Kingdom known to the world. "And of them he chose twelve, whom he named apostles."

It is not difficult to visualize the Lord with a large crowd of rough, hard-working people clustered about Him. Motioning for everyone to be quiet, He quickly calls out the names of Peter, Andrew, James, John, Philip, Bartholomew, Matthew, Thomas, James the son of Alphaeus, Simon, Judas the brother of James, and Judas Iscariot.

Some of these men had already become intimate friends and bosom companions of Jesus but now the time had come to bind them together in a solid organization. This was the occasion when they were to receive their official appointments. Prior to this event they had been "disciples" but henceforth they were to be known as "the twelve".

This was the birthday of the Church.

No doubt many questions surged through the minds of these men as they retired from the multitude to receive instructions concerning their special calling. First of all they learned that they were to be designated by the term "apostles", a Greek word meaning "ambassadors to be sent".

On this momentous occasion the Christian Church was founded. Jesus literally carved the first nucleus of members out of rugged humanity of the fishermen type. "I will make you fishers of men," said He.

Up until this time the Jews had watched Jesus closely. Many of the leaders thought that perhaps He would start a revolution, stir up a mob, organize an army, drive Caesar from the throne and give temporal power to Israel. True, great crowds were following the young Teacher from Galilee. Multitudes crowded in on all sides to hear His words. Miracles were being performed.

Would He take the next step and lead a revolt against the Romans? If He had done this, the Jews would have accepted Him as Messiah instead of demanding His death.

Now that He had selected the men who were to help Him, the next thing was to make a public declaration of religious principles and give the Church its charter. Thousands of men and women were assembled on the rocky summit of a mountain awaiting His arrival. Coming before this vast audience with the twelve He began to expound the philosophy and formulate the principles of love, with which He proposed to eventually conquer the world.

He preached the Sermon on the Mount. His words seemed to drip with honey. The people were profoundly moved but the Jewish leaders were not at all impressed. He taught love and they believed in hate. He condemned selfishness and they were selfish to the core of their hearts. He, therefore, failed utterly to fit into their distorted Messianic ideals. He made no charges against the Romans nor did He seek to stir up the rabble against the Gentiles.

After laying down the fundamental principles of the Church in His address on the Beatitudes, Jesus continued by explaining the position that His organization was to occupy in the world.

"Ye are the salt of the earth," He said. "Ye are the light of the world."

At that time, religion consisted chiefly in external ordinances and formal observances. Jesus faced the task of showing thick-headed materialistic human beings the necessity of translating their religious beliefs into heart purity and holy living. He knew that neither the mythology of the Greeks and Romans or the cold ritualism of the Jews could prepare souls for eternity.

His next pronouncement therefore opened a wound between Judaism and Christianity which has not been healed until this day. Here are His words, "Except your righteousness shall exceed the righteousness of the scribes and Pharisees, ye shall in no case enter into the Kingdom of heaven".

That statement ended it as far as the Jewish leaders were concerned! By this time their false Messianic hopes in Him had not only vanished, but they had turned to become His bitterest enemies.

Referring to the Old Testament law, Jesus sought to make the people understand that heart impulses count most, that character depends upon man's heart attitude toward God and his fellowman. "Ye have heard it said by them of old time, Thou shalt not kill; and whosoever shall kill shall be in danger of the judgment: But I say unto you, That whosoever is angry with his brother without cause shall be in danger of the judgment."

In other words, the inner tendency of a man's nature toward evil does not have to manifest itself in a physical act in order to become sin. The condition of the heart is what counts!

Jesus, in the Sermon on the Mount, was introducing two major ideals—(1) love is the mightiest force in the universe and (2) religion is a thing of the heart instead of an outward, physical observance. These were the principles which the Church was charged, on this eventful occasion, to give to the world.

No time was lost by the little Church in starting out to fulfill its mission. These men were quick to catch the vision. The twelve were sent out two by two, on a missionary tour that took them over Galilee where they expounded the new, transforming message in all the towns and villages. At a later time thirty-five more pairs, making a total of seventy men, were sent forth to sound the same clarion call. Jesus told them, "Behold, I send you forth as sheep in the midst of wolves".

Meanwhile, the Jewish Messianic complex insisted on asserting itself among the Galilean crowds. They wanted a king. They had it in their heads that they were going to rule over the Gentiles. Being unable to grasp the spiritual significance of the Lord's message and being circumscribed by blind nationalism, the rabble—not the leaders—were determined to make Him their King.

Jesus killed this movement in the borning. Throughout His earth-life He made it clear that "My Kingdom is not of this world". He was unwilling to have His work degenerate to the level of the many other Messiahs who had appeared in Israel from time to time.

He also knew that even if the crown of the Jews was to be placed upon His head, it would have no value in the presence of the Gentile nations scattered around them. Moreover, He had no desire to come under the old out-grown scheme of government which was being administered by scheming, tricky Jewish leaders. Finally, such an arrangement would fail to fulfill the Old Testament prophecies which pointed to the death, resurrection, and ultimate triumph of His efforts along spiritual lines.

For these and other reasons Jesus refused to allow Himself to be exploited by the Jews who were cursed with a warped and inflated idea of their nation's superiority in temporal matters.

As the months rolled by and the apostles had been given an opportunity to learn the details of Christ's plan of world conquest, the time finally came when they were to hear from His own lips a statement of doctrine that was to become the permanent and fixed corner-stone of the new institution which He was building on the earth.

The occasion was a rendezvous on the coast of Caesarea Philippi where the little travelling Church had paused for a few days.

Referring to the rumors which were being circulated about Him, He inquired, "Whom do men say that I the Son of man am?" Several answers were forthcoming. Some people were saying that He was John the Baptist, and others Elijah. One report was being circulated that He was Jeremiah, the weeping prophet, returned to earth.

"But who say ye that I am?"

It was Peter who answered, "Thou art the Christ, the Son of the living God". And Jesus replied, "Upon this rock I will build my church; and the gates of hell shall not prevail against it".

There can be no question that when Christ used the metaphor "rock" that He was referring to His deity.

The Church's one foundation,
  Is Jesus Christ her Lord;
She is the new creation,
  By water and the blood;
From heaven He came and sought her
  To be His holy bride,
With His own blood He bought her,
  And for her life He died.

By analogy, the mind turns back to another rock—the rock which Moses smote during Israel's desert wanderings. Camp had been pitched at Rephidim but there was no water to drink. Lips were parched, mouths were dry, death stared the people in the face.

Through an act of supernatural intervention Moses was directed to smite the rock in Horeb, and as he did so, there gushed from it a crystal flow of sparkling water in the desert. The thirst of everyone was quenched.

In like manner, the twelve were shown a great rock of truth. The smitten-rock in Horeb was a type of the smitten-body of Christ. Paul had this in mind when he wrote to the Church at Corinth, "And did all drink the same spiritual drink; for they drank of that spiritual Rock that followed them: and that Rock was Christ".

The next crisis in Church history took place at the Jewish harvest feast which was called Pentecost, in the year 29 A.D. This event marked the inauguration of their program on a world-wide scale.

When some of the apostles became too eager and anxious to have the Kingdom of God ushered in while Christ was yet with them, they were told, "It is not for you to know the times or the seasons." But Jesus had been careful to instruct them to wait in Jerusalem until there should come upon them a special baptism of spiritual power. "Ye shall receive power",

He said, "after that the Holy Ghost is come upon you: and ye shall be witnesses unto me both in Jerusalem, and in all Judaea, and in Samaria, and unto the uttermost part of the earth".

So when the curtain raised on the great drama of Pentecost a group of bold men stepped forward whose mental horizons had been pushed back. They saw far beyond the cramped nationalism of Jewry—they looked out to the ends of the earth, down the vista of the centuries, and realized that the precious Gospel was not to be confined to any single sect, color or nationality. The scales had been lifted from their eyes and now they saw that the ministry of the Church was for the "whole world".

This was a new doctrine, a revolutionary ideal, a pernicious teaching to the narrow-minded Jewish leaders who believed that only Israel was favored in the sight of the Almighty.

The parting words of the Christ to go out and evangelize the nations, uttered just before His ascension, had served to stimulate the entire Church membership, which by this time numbered a few hundred. About one hundred and twenty of these early Christians went at once to the upper room where the apostles had been making their headquarters in Jerusalem. Here they prayed and tarried for the coming of the Spirit. Certain business matters were also looked after which included the selecting of Matthias to replace Judas Iscariot as a member of the apostolic band. Judas had committed suicide.

"And when the day of Pentecost was fully come, they were all with one accord in one place. And suddenly there came a sound from heaven as of a rushing mighty wind, and it filled all the house where they were sitting."

The streets of Jerusalem were crowded with milling masses of anxious visitors from Egypt, Asia Minor,

Italy and other places. Many of these out-of-town guests had heard reports about the strange things that had been happening in Jerusalem during the last few months. They were eager to know the truth about the Nazarene and the peculiar people who were following Him. They wanted to see these strange creatures who were said to be turning the world upside down. The visiting multitudes had been told many colorful and fantastic stories and now they hoped to see and hear for themselves.

Imagine their delight when they heard that considerable excitement was being started by the little Church over at the foot of Mount Moriah, the site on which the Temple stood. Now that the apostles were appearing in public, they too would be able to observe the workings of the new Church movement and would be able to carry reports back to their friends and neighbors at home.

But not every visitor was actuated by mere curiosity and fanaticism. Thousands were serious, earnest Jews who approached the matter with open minds. What they wanted above everything else was dependable information.

The members of the Church knew that this afforded a truly great opportunity to scatter the message which Jesus had admonished them to declare to the "uttermost part of the earth". If these people, or a considerable number of them could be won over to their side, they would hasten back to their respective communities and become living torches for the purpose of lighting new spiritual fires. But there was no time to be lost. The Pentecostal celebration would soon be drawing to a close. The apostles and their helpers were determined to reach the largest number of people in the shortest possible time.

After the melting experience in the upper room, the hundred and twenty moved down through the narrow streets to where the throngs of people were scattered around the temple area and public places. They immediately began to shout about the marvelous words and miraculous works of the Nazarene who had healed sick people, cleansed lepers, raised the dead, forgiven sins—how He had been put to death by wicked Jews, had come out of the new tomb which belonged to a rich man by the name of Joseph, whose home was in Arimathaea—how the risen Christ had appeared to scores of people and shown Himself by "many infallible proofs", and was at last swept up into heaven after making the solemn declaration that He would some day come back again.

Here stood John hurriedly addressing a group, there was James, over yonder was Philip. Everybody was listening with wide-eyed amazement. It is easy to understand how such an evangelistic message as the Church was then declaring, would burn its way into the calloused hearts of the hearers. Moreover, there seemed to be a mellow glow of divine light surrounding the faces of all the speakers, and their words fell with a strange eloquence upon the ears of everyone who heard.

Some were instantly converted. Others were favorably impressed but not to the point of making immediate decisions. Some were reticent, and still others scoffed saying, "These men are full of new wine". To the mockers who thus sneered, a certain apostle replied, with demolishing sarcasm, that it was too early in the day for anybody to be drunk.

Then came the Pentecostal oration by Peter, the loyal spokesman who had previously declared the deity of Christ in the conversation that took place on the coast of Caesarea Philippi.

The tricky Jews had thought that once the life of Christ could be taken, the little Church would soon disband and the new movement would die. Who can imagine their disappointment and disillusionment when in one single day they saw five thousand people definitely converted, ready to embrace the doctrines of the Christ!

Having failed to crush the movement by killing its Leader, they next took counsel as to how best proceed in an attempt to destroy the apostles. They were badly handicapped, however, by the fact that some of their own leaders were being converted, while others, like Gamaliel, were refusing to join in the persecution by advocating a "hands off" policy.

Millions of sermons have been preached since Peter delivered his famous message at Pentecost but none have equaled it for power, unction, logic and effectiveness. "Ye men of Israel, hear these words", he shouted, "Jesus of Nazareth, a man approved of God among you by miracles and wonders and signs, which God did by him in the midst of you, as ye yourselves also know: Him, being delivered by the determinate counsel and fore-knowledge of God, ye have taken, and by wicked hands have crucified and slain: Whom God hath raised up, having loosed the pains of death: because it was not possible that he should be holden of it."

In substance, this was the same message that Peter had expressed in his remark to Jesus, "Thou art the Christ, the Son of the living God". In other words, the theme of Peter's Pentecostal address was THE DIETY OF CHRIST. And this was the "Rock" upon which Christ had said He was going to build His Church.

At Pentecost, Peter smote this great "Rock" of truth and a pure crystal stream of living water came flowing out to flow through the centuries, as truly as water gushed from the smitten rock in Horeb to quench the thirst of the Children of Israel during their desert experiences.

This mighty current, the Church of Jesus Christ, has poured through nineteen hundred years of human history and has reached as our Lord said, to the "uttermost part of the earth".

It is probable that if some of the members of the little Church at Pentecost had known what awaited them—the pain, the suffering, the persecution and bloodshed, that the future held in store—they would have been less zealous and might have even faltered and turned back.

THE SUFFERING

ONE of the most sordid stories of history relates to the intrigue of the Jews, who having failed in killing the infant Church, began influencing pagans to acts of violence against the early Christians. The Roman law forbade the starting of new religions and this became a weapon for inciting the passions of the people against the apostles and their helpers. Truly, Jesus had sent His followers out as sheep among wolves—such was the hardness of human hearts toward the things of God.

During the first few centuries of the Church's existence the Jews constantly stirred up Gentile officials against Christians. They passed no opportunity to pour oil on the flames of persecution.

So we see that the struggling Christians encountered hostility from three different sources: (1) The natural prejudice of the pagans who regarded the Church as an encroachment upon their mythology, (2) the Roman government which sought to squelch anything in the way of a new departure from the established forms of religious observance, and (3) the vicious hatred of the Jews who feared that the new faith might become the undoing of Judaism.

The fact that the Church should have endured such powerfully entrenched opposition and lived through these scenes of bloody torture testifies to its spiritual vitality and divine leadership. It took centuries for its enemies to learn that they could not destroy spiritual truth with physical weapons.

After its first encounter with the Jews, the next great wave of slaughter broke loose under Nero who was Emperor of the Roman Empire from A. D. 54 to 68. The original family name of this fiend was L. Domitius Ahenobarbus. He was born in A. D. 37. Paul was one of the thousands of Christians trapped in this awful spasm of persecution.

Once Nero's appetite for human blood had been whetted, there was no stopping him until his dastardly crime wave could run its course and exhaust itself in human suffering. Not only did he put Christians to death by the tens of thousands but he also tortured and killed many of his most intimate friends and relatives. After five years on the throne he became literally intoxicated with the power that he possessed.

Conceiving himself to be both a great musician and poet, he decided to write a poem on the destruction of Troy. In order to secure graphic inspiration for the ode he decided to set the city of Rome on fire the night of July 18, 64. The conflagration roared fiercely for six days and when it seemed to be dying down, it broke out afresh in another section until the entire city was destroyed.

When reports leaked out that Nero himself was responsible for the tragedy, he did the pitiless thing of placing the blame upon the Christians. Hatred rose throughout the Roman Empire which resulted in a pogrom that caused believers to again be hunted like animals. Forgetting Nero for the time being, the people focused their attacks upon powerless Christians everywhere.

Concerning this period of suffering, one writer on Church history says, "Some Christians were sewn up in the skins of wild beasts, to be torn to pieces by dogs; others were crucified; a part of them were smeared with pitch and then set on fire, serving as torches to illuminate the Emperor's gardens. Paul the apostle was dragged out of his cell, brought before the imperial tribunal, and condemned to death. Because he was a Roman citizen he was allowed to suffer the more respectable death of the sword. The great leader of the twelve, the apostle Peter, was also caught in Nero's drag-net and crucified head down.

"Although we have no definite records, it may be safely taken for granted that several of the other apostles and leading evangelists suffered martyrdom on this occasion, for though the persecution in its most violent form was limited to Rome and its immediate surroundings, the effect of it was felt in all the provinces, and hostile governors were quick to vent their spleen upon the helpless Nazarenes.

"Tacitus, great Roman historian and contemporary of Nero, tells us that although the Christians were generally despised, yet the tortures inflicted upon them by Nero were so intrinsically devilish that a general feeling of pity was aroused."

To defray the expense of rebuilding Rome, Nero had Italy and all Roman provinces systematically ransacked. After the first violent storm of persecution passed, the feeling began to sink in upon the people that the presence of the miserable Christians in Rome was responsible for the curse which had come upon the Empire. The gods had been provoked! Therefore it became a patriotic service to slay a Christian. Strange as it may seem, Christians of this era were regarded as atheists because they refused to subscribe to the doctrines of either Judaism or Roman and Grecian mythology. All public disasters such as famines and earthquakes were credited to the Christians by the superstitious Romans.

In spite of his brutality, Nero was at heart a cringing coward. In every crisis, his fear complex became an obsession with him. His wild, insane life came to an end in A. D. 68 when the Roman Senate sentenced him to die. In a spasm of mental torment, beside himself with fear, he committed suicide at the age of 31, having ruled Rome 14 years.

With his death, the line of the Caesars ended and Roman imperialism entered a new phase. Nero's statues were broken, his name was everywhere erased, and his "golden house" demolished. Many Christians of that period believed he was the mystic Antichrist prophecied all through the Bible to come, just before the second coming of Christ, to torture the saints.

Quick on the heels of the Neronian persecution came the next slaughter under Emperor Domitan and his successor Trajan. It is almost unbelievable that the Church could have lived through these trials but every outburst of violence became a confirmation of the truth that "the blood of martyrs is the seed of the Church". All a Christian had to do to save his life was to deny Jesus Christ. And this, countless thousands refused to do!

Among the many who perished under Trajan during the close of the first century and the beginning of the second, were Simeon a distant relative of Jesus and Bishop of Jerusalem, and Ignatius the Bishop of Antioch. Both died horrible deaths. Simeon was crucified. Ignatius was fed to lions for public entertainment.

In the middle of the second century Marcus Aurelius came to the throne. He was a pagan through and through. If the security of the Empire depends upon winning the favor of the deities he reasoned, and if Christianity is opposed to the mythology of the gods, then it must be pleasing to the gods to blot Christians from existence.

Moreover, Aurelius learned that the Church possessed a book, a strange mystical document, called the Apocalypse, which purported to unveil the future. One of their number, a man by the name of John, was supposed to have compiled it out of visions which he had received while banished on the Isle of Patmos. It was said to be a book on prophecy which, among other things, described the fall of the Roman Empire.

What more was needed to convict the Christians of circulating pernicious ideas inimical to the welfare of the nation? And again the blood of the most righteous people on the face of the earth began to flow!

Polycarp, Bishop of Smyrna, who in years past had been a disciple of John the Revelator, was among those destroyed by the blood-thirsty Aurelius. This martyr was burned at the stake for refusing to recant. Justin Martyr, another warrior of the faith, was put to death during this period for refusing to burn incense to a heathen deity.

Soon after this, a wave of violence broke out in northern Africa under Severus who ruled Rome during the latter part of the second century and the beginning of the third. Like his predecessors he was hard and cruel in his dealings with the Church.

Particular attention is called to two young Christian women whose deaths at this time were as heroic as those of any men who ever sacrificed their lives for the Master. Their names were Felicitas and Perpetua.

The stations in life from which these two people came serve to illustrate how the spirit of Christianity was beginning to permeate all classes by this time. Felicitas was a slave and Perpetua was of noble birth.

Only a few days before she was to die for her Lord, Felicitas gave birth to a child. Vulgar soldiers, who were allowed to witness the scene of her travail, said sneeringly, "If you cannot bear this, what will you do when the wild cows take you on their horns three days from now?" She is quoted as replying, "This I am bearing alone; later there will be One within me to suffer for me because I am sacrificing myself for Him".

During this time the winsome Perpetua was languishing in prison with her nursing child at her breasts. Even the entreaties of her aged father could not swerve her from the course she was pursuing and cause her to recant. "All is in God's hands", she told him.

She was one of a group of Christian prisoners to be sentenced for doing missionary work. The men were condemned to death by being cast to the lions, bears, and leopards; the women were sentenced to die among the wild cows. A writer of Church history describes her death as follows: "Perpetua seemed to be in a trance when she made her appearance, and when the furious cow was through with her she was still alive. In accordance with custom a young gladiator was sent into the open arena to put a finish to her with a sword. He struck her a glancing blow. Then, with her own hand, she directed the sword to a vital spot and told the youth to go ahead. Another soul had been released."

But no matter the ingenious methods employed by both Jews and pagans in trying to exterminate Christianity, the new faith not only survived, it actually prospered. There is no way of explaining how this could be—how the Church could thrive on persecution —except by the fact that it is builded upon a "Rock," the fulfillment of its Founder's promise, "the gates of hell shall not prevail against it".

At length, the vitality of the Church became such

a powerful influence that in the early part of the fourth century we find a Christian Emperor—Constantine—ascending to the throne of Rome. He introduced many reforms and laws designed to protect Christians. At last, after three full centuries of merciless torture, the Church was to get a square deal. At last, Christians could pray and testify without expecting to be killed for it!

There were ten definite stages to the program of persecution which had been endured. Historians are generally agreed that the carnival of misery through which the Church passed during the first three centuries is divided into ten sections or epochs. And this fulfilled the prediction given by Jesus through the lips of John in Revelation 2:10, "Fear none of those things which thou shalt suffer: behold, the devil shall cast some of you into prison, that ye may be tried; and ye shall have tribulation TEN DAYS: be thou faithful unto death, and I will give thee a crown of life".

The Greek word in the original text which is translated *day* in the above passage does not necessarily mean twenty-four hours. It is *hemera* which may refer to a "period of time", or a number of years.

Beyond doubt the "ten days" of Revelation 2:10 pointed prophetically to the ten successive periods of suffering through which the Church was destined to pass.

THE REFORMER

CONSTANTINE was sincere but he never fully succeeded in grasping the true content of Christianity. His pagan past influenced all that he said and did. But he walked in the light that he possessed.

Having turned his back upon the ancient mythologies, it is not difficult to understand why his revolutionary methods should have created so much dissension within his Kingdom. He became one of the most unpopular men in the city of Rome.

The strain on his popularity became such that he actually shunned Rome and spent most of his time in other parts of the Empire. By degrees there was built up in his mind an exalted conception of a truly Christian city and he decided to build it—a community that would reflect the spirit of the new religion which he had embraced. With Constantine, to think was to act. He was a man of firm conviction, undaunted courage and an iron will.

Traveling some seven hundred miles east of Rome, he selected the site for his "ideal city" on the ruins of the old city of Byzantium. Here he built, from the ground up, Constantinople, which is now known as Istanbul. No pagan temples were allowed within its borders; numerous Christian Churches were erected. Constantine himself examined the Scriptures with great care and even tried his hand at preaching occasionally. During his reign, paganism became *taboo!*

What a turn-about-face the Roman government had made!

But the Christianity of Constantine's era was wholly unlike the Christianity of the days of the apostles. Three hundred years of suffering had left its mark. The spiritual momentum of Pentecost was lost to a great degree. And in brushing against paganism, Christianity had taken on some of its idolatry and mythology. Pagan temples, priests and soothsayers had had a bad influence on the cause of Christ.

These Satanic influences, which so weakened Christianity, were prophecied by the Lord in His outline of Church history as sketched in the thirteenth Chapter of Matthew. Seven parables are recorded, each of which deals with the growth, development and posterity of the new spiritual conception which He had introduced into the world. The story of the mustard seed provides particularly for the polluting effect of paganism and other forms of heresy in their contact with Christianity.

"Another parable put he forth unto them, saying, The kingdom of heaven is like to a grain of mustard seed, which a man took, and sowed in his field: Which indeed is the least of all seeds: but when it is grown, it is the greatest among herbs, and becometh a tree, so that the birds of the air come and lodge in the branches thereof."

The huge mustard bush starts with a small beginning, a tiny, infinitesimal seed. It grows into a large tree. In like manner, the Church began with only twelve members but by the time of Constantine its membership had increased to millions, reaching as far east as the borders of modern Afghanistan, as far west as the western coasts of what is now Ireland, covering France and Spain, as far north as Poland and Germany, and as far south as the Sahara Desert. Roughly, this was the boundary line of the Roman Empire at that time but the influence of Christianity was felt even beyond this territory.

A mustard bush has many branches. In like manner, the power of the Church was felt in many directions, touching every type of human being and every phase of daily life.

Birds of the air could lodge and build nests in a mustard tree. This part of the parable refers to the presence of demons building their nests, being harbored within the confines, of the Church. The Devil's work in bringing internal evils into the Church is symbolized by the birds lodging in its branches.

It is tragic to realize to what extent Christianity had imbibed the spirit of paganism by the time of Constantine's appearance. There was a commingling of mythological philosophy and Christian doctrine. Precious spiritual truths, revealed through the apostles, were interpreted in terms of vulgar ceremonies and pagan practices. The most concrete and visible evidence of this deterioration is to be seen in the prevalency of idols.

Believers in Grecian and Roman mythologies cast their conceptions of the deities who were supposed to operate the universe, into the moulds of idols made of stone and wood. It is a long story how this idolatry had been handed down to them from ancient Babylon and through the Egyptians. Nevertheless the perverting influence upon the Church was terrific. It resulted in all manner of liberties, heresies and weird practices being introduced in the name of Christianity and under the ensign of the cross. In some respects one could hardly realize that this was the same institution that had precipitated the great tidal wave of divine power at Pentecost.

It would be a mistake, however, to convey the impression that paganism wielded a greater influence than Christianity. The exact opposite is true. For instance, neither Judaism or mythology succeeded in impregnating the Roman mind with any kind of moral idealism. It remained for the Christians, by their exemplary lives and refined teachings, to prick the conscience, condemn licentiousness and place restraint upon the immorality of the citizenry of the Empire.

This is another reason why the believers were so thoroughly hated—by their teachings and interpretation of the sacred Scriptures they interfered with the carnal indulgences of those about them. The attitude of Christians in refusing to attend Roman games, entertainments and patriotic celebrations because of the immorality of these occasions, was another cause for hostility.

Constantine died at the age of sixty-four. He was

succeeded by his three sons Constantine II, Constans and Constantius. They were all favorable to the Church but shared the popular views of the time which involved a blending of paganism with Christianity. Idolatry and kindred evils continued to invade the Church with ever increasing intensity.

The mustard tree continued to grow but the birds remained in the branches. In the year A.D. 346 there was born a child upon whose shoulders the burden of the Roman government was destined to rest heavily. He became Emperor Theodosius. Like Constantine he sought to promote the interests of the Church by the power of the sword. His period of reign ended during the latter part of the fourth century. Concentrating his efforts largely upon Egypt he sought to blot paganism from that part of the world. By this time the tables had completely turned and now it was the pagans, not the Christians, who were on the defensive.

Theodosius razed pagan temples to the ground. By a royal edict he ordered every temple in the city of Alexandria destroyed, including Bacchus, a gorgeous building which housed the idol of Serapis. This figment of pagan imagination was a creation of enormous proportions laden with gems, jewels, silver and gold.

The people had been taught by the priests to believe that if this idol was ever destroyed the world would come to an end by falling to pieces. Defying tradition, the Emperor ordered it smashed. The pagans of Alexandria were struck with horror. Great crowds looked on with anxiety as a daring worker climbed a ladder, raised a sledge, and knocked the idol's face to smithereens.

To their amazement the earth did not begin to reel and crack open. When the massive head of the god rolled to the floor, swarms of rats poured out of it, rushing in all directions. Multitudes of pagans were instantly disillusioned and there was a great turning to Christianity as a result of this incident.

The voices of several truly great preachers, men of God, began to be heard above the din and babble of paganized Christian confusion. Among these was Saint Augustine who was born in the middle of the fourth century. His official position was that of Bishop of Hippo, Africa.

His father, a dissolute pagan, professed conversion before his death. His mother, Monnica, was revered as one of the most holy and devout women of Church history. As a young man Augustine lived a wild life of dissipation but the prayers of his saintly mother followed him even when he roamed the paths of sin. Her intercession is credited by all Church historians as being the cause of his conversion. Once he found Christ to be his Savior, he turned to the Gospel and Christian service with the same zeal and earnestness that he had served Satan.

Augustine was blessed with an unusual intellect. What we know today as Roman Catholicism was just beginning to get a firm grip upon the masses and Augustine became an ascetic, renounced all worldly affairs and became what we would now call a monk. He served as Bishop of Hippo for thirty-five years. He wrote over one thousand manuscripts, the two most important theological books being, "The City of God" and "Confessions".

Though highly exalted by his prominence in religious affairs, yet he led a life of extreme simplicity and self-denial. The charm and sweetness of his disposition was an inspiration to all who knew him. At a time when the clouds of spiritual darkness were beginning to form throughout the civilized world, Augustine stands like a bright light on a dark background. He possessed much of the spirit and vision of the apostles. He went to his heavenly reward in A.D. 430.

In 395 the Roman Empire divided into eastern and western sections. The year 476 witnessed the fall of the western branch at the hands of the barbarians. The eastern division stood until 1453 when the Turks conquered Constantinople.

The fifth century witnessed a Church membership numbering into the millions, a gorgeous type of architecture, images, idols, altars, pagan ritualism and heathen practices—all in the name of Christ and Christianity. The original apostolic purity appears to have been almost entirely lost. A missionary spirit was wholly lacking. There was no emotional warmth. The clammy hand of paganism had destroyed spiritual vitality. There existed "a form of godliness denying the power thereof."

Then here came the Vandals from the north. The city of Rome was sacked. Churches were destroyed. Roman civilization, root and branch, was destroyed. Europe plunged into a night of dark ages which continued for about one thousand years. The so-called Church fought for its life—and won.

Religious leaders felt that a central government was sorely needed in order to correlate Christian activity and to direct Church affairs from one center. "In union" they believed "there is strength." Prior to the coming of the Vandals, the strongest religious nerve-center of the Christians had been established in the city of Rome. In reality, Rome was the seat of the Church. So when the leaders got together to form a united body, Rome automatically became the headquarters. And the chief patriarch was called the "papa"— the Pope.

After several years of chaos, the Church raised its head above the turmoil as the most perfectly organized body in the world. The Pope, being its leader, was therefore vested with ever increasing powers. As the leaders came together in an organized body, a gap was produced between higher and lower classes. Education came to be more and more concentrated with the clergy while the common people became increasingly ignorant.

A selfish pagan priesthood found it advantageous to keep the people in darkness and superstition. Chains of ignorance were therefore deliberately forged upon the masses and the Bible was kept from them. The office of the Pope became the world's most powerful force and heads of governments frequently cringed under the lash of its incumbents.

From 590 to 604 Gregory I occupied the Papal throne and under his reign the Church headquarters at Rome became increasingly powerful in temporal matters pertaining to State affairs. Other Popes followed in his path and before a great while all the nations of western Europe were subservient to them.

Another thing that served to bring Christians together in a united mass were the attacks of the Mohammedans from the outside. The geographical source of this opposition was the Arabian desert where a religious fanatic by the name of Mohammed was born in the year 570.

He was a nervous individual, given to epileptic fits and mental hallucinations. He taught that Christ was a good Man but out of date. Mohammed was exalted to a superior rank because he was supposed to be a later incarnation of deity. His dreams, visions and teachings were written in a book called the Koran. He claimed to trace his ancestry in a straight line back to Ishmael, the illegitimate son of Abraham.

Under the teachings of Mohammed, the standard of women was reduced to the level of beasts. The Koran teaches polygamy and advocates immorality as a sure road to heaven. According to Mohammed it was a service to God, a step on the pathway upward, to take the life of a Christian. In other words, Mohammedanism embodies and sanctifies all the fierceness and terror for which desert life is noted.

Hordes of wild, frenzied human beings, bent on

plunder and rapacity, swept against the nations of the west determined to destroy everything bearing the least semblance of Christianity. The Mohammedan wars continued for about one hundred years in different part of the world. It looked for a time as though Europe was doomed to come under the bloody claws of Islam. Closer and closer did the troops of Allah push until finally they reached the borders of France.

Because the Mohammedans gained complete control of the east, the Church lost its grip in that part of the world. When the western Church was likewise threatened with ruin, the Christians suddenly took on new courage and helped their rulers as they routed the intruders. The battle at Tours in 732 was the turning point. On that occasion Charles Martel, King of France, led the victorious forces and put up the line of defense that blocked the advance of Allah and saved Europe.

Tours is situated less than two hundred miles southwest of Paris. For seven days the two armies stood facing each other before the fighting actually began. It was the moral and physical superiority of the Teutonic race, coupled with a spirit of real Christian daring, that won the day and sent the Moslems back home. Pacensis, the historian, declares that the Arab cavalry broke before the "immovable wall' of the Frankish soldiers who stood as firm "as a rock of ice."

Out of Europe's centuries of boiling turmoil, the succession of Popes emerged stronger and stronger. When the year 800 arrived we find an almost omnipotent State Church. This was the year that Charlemagne of France came to Rome to be crowned Emperor of all the Romans by Pope Leo III. Thus, the Holy Roman Empire, a religious-political mechanism, was invented. Charlemagne did wonders for the Church as far as increasing its power in temporal matters was concerned. He died in the year 814.

The Holy Roman Empire, working in conjunction with the Church, became an indomitable combination. As the heads of governments weakened, the Church became increasingly strong and increasingly worldly— thus moving further and further from the original apostolic ideal.

Finally, with the coming of Pope Hildebrand, the corrupt system unblushingly exalted itself above all governments and openly declared that henceforth it would be supreme in both spiritual and temporal affairs. From this time on the Papacy stood ready to crush any nation or official who dared to oppose its iron will. With the developing of this great apostasy, the Church departed entirely from the mission that Jesus outlined for it to achieve. Moreover, the pagan practices and heresies which had increased steadily on the inside of the organization served to destroy its spiritual power without restraint.

What would the Founder of the Church have said had He been on earth when Hildebrand required Emperor Henry IV to knuckle before him, begging for mercy, standing barefooted in the snow three days and nights, for having violated the Papal wishes! When the Pope at last granted him an audience, Henry threw and with bitter tears streaming down his face, pleaded, his strong, tall figure on the floor at Hildebrand's feet "Grant me thy absolution"!

Looking back through the centuries, we can see how far Christianity had departed from its primal purity in becoming a paganized, State religion. A well known student of Church history remarks, "Out of these circumstances grew the extensive use of images in the churches, the multitudinous accounts of fantastic miracles, and the great passion for relics. Among the thousands of relics in the churches and monasteries those of Jesus and his mother were naturally regarded as the most precious of all. The trouble was that there was too great an abundance of them. The seamless coat of Jesus was found in several places; there were a great number of fragments of the manger in which the baby Jesus had lain, of the cross on which he was nailed, of the bread which the Master gave to his disciples, etc. There were also portions of mother Mary's milk, of her hair, her dress, and her cloak. The head of John the Baptist was preserved and venerated in numerous places at the same time. Great church festivals were often held in connection with these relics, and the multitude used to lie kneeling before them in wide-eyed wonderment."

These outrages and insane observances show how far and fast the Church was drifting from its original position. How long before a reaction could be expected to take place? How long before it would encounter defiant, spiritual opposition? How long before the black cloud of paganism's night would be lifted?

Idol worship was one of the chief curses of this period of Church history. One of the early reformers is quoted as saying that he "made an investigation of the relics situation, and found almost a shipload of the cross and so many teeth of mother Mary that the poor woman must have had the head of a monster".

The eleventh century found the Turks a Mohammedan kingdom. Christians who wanted to make pilgrimages to the Holy Land went at the risk of their lives. Thousands were slaughtered. These trials revived the old feud between the followers of Christ and the followers of Allah. Many bloody struggles ensued with the result that the Mohammedans relaxed their grip on the homeland of Jesus. Papal banners eventually flew over Jerusalem, Jericho, Bethlehem and other places in Bible lands. These wars were known as the Crusades. But before many years passed, the Turks again sacked the Holy Land.

The dignitaries of the Church had become increasingly intolerant ever since the days of Constantine. When the curtain lifted on the fourteenth century, it revealed a Church filled with sin of every form, torn by dissension, wounded by war and utterly devoid of spiritual power. Inner struggles were such that as many as three Popes were sometimes ruling simultaneously. Church doctrines had become so perverted that the apostles would have scarcely been able to recognize the institution which they died to help establish.

Take for example, the sale of "indulgences"—a plan vitally related to the solution of the sin problem. Every human being whose conscience is normal is aware of his short-comings, human weaknesses, and wrong doings. Where there is a sense of guilt for a sin committed there is always an accompanying feeling of remorse. Because every human being possesses a religious instinct by nature, we find people resorting to all sorts of practices in their attempts to pacify the conscience. The Roman Church saw an opportunity to "cash in" on this instinct through the sale of indulgences.

The practice was adopted of imposing a penalty for every sin confessed. Some sort of self-inflicted punishment and humiliation was required to accompany the confession. Instead of repentance being a thing of the heart, an experience in the inner life, it was made an outward act, something the penitent had to *do*.

Having thus established this premise, namely that salvation resulted from *good works*, the rest was easy. A man will do anything to set himself free from the terrors of sin! So, Churchmen introduced the scheme of buying soul rest and freedom from guilt by paying certain sums of money. They told the poor, ignorant, struggling masses that instead of inflicting suffering upon themselves for sins committed, they could purchase an indulgence by paying into the coffers of the Church. In the beginning it was taught that only a part of one's sins could thus be atoned for, later that the entire sin could be wiped out, and finally that future sins could be cared for by making proper payments. In other words, put a shekel in the money-box and do as you please for the next three months.

Anyone can see how such a system would give license to carnal depravity. Is it any wonder that the few leaders who were spiritually minded should have risen in revolt? Little did the ruling leaders realize that this was the straw that would break the camel's back and shake the apostate ecclesiastical system down to its mudsills.

(Parenthetically, I might remark that on a recent visit to Paris I saw indulgences being provided for sins yet to be committed as I walked through the historic Notre Dame Cathedral. Church officials had placed bulletins around the altars explaining that by prayerfully kneeling in front of an idol and lighting a candle, the sins of the next one hundred days could be atoned for. The money-box was close by.)

This ancient plan caused large sums of money to pour into the Church treasury. It was decidedly a paying proposition. If the finances were low in Rome, if a new church edifice was to be built, or if some other emergency came up, all the Pope had to do was to send a group of "salesmen" out to scour the country with indulgences. It was a pretty arrangement! But certain men called "Reformers" began to cry out against this and other evil practices which had crept into the Church. These men were equally vehement in denouncing the leaders of Rome, and the priesthood in general, for their personal sins and licentious ways of living. The "Protesters" increased rapidly both in numbers and influence.

Pope Leo X, a young man only thirty-seven years old, was elected March 11, 1513. Within four years from the time he took the Papal throne, the Reformation broke upon the world. Those who dared to *protest* against the evils of Churchanity, oppose the sale of indulgences, demand an open Bible for the masses, call for a spiritual revival in the Church that would bring it back to apostolic purity—such people were called heretics and Protestants—because they were Protesters. Tens of thousands of courageous saints were put to death in an orgy of killing which in some respects equalled the persecution of first-century believers.

Most of the leaders of the Reformation advocated moderate measures to merely purge and improve the Holy See at Rome. Others, however, demanded the destruction of the entire system so that something new and better could be built from the ground up. William Occam, John of Jandun and Marsilius of Padua were leading voices among the latter group. These men were scholars who knew how to sway the masses and blaze trails for better days.

Over in England things had been boiling for a long time, thanks to the efforts of John Wyclif who made a great contribution to public enlightenment by translating the Bible into the English language as Luther later translated it into German. Wyclif wrote about two hundred books. His daring independence made him a harbinger of the Reformation, a pioneer and leader for those who were to follow later. What Wyclif was to England, John Huss was to Bohemia.

Such men as these were helping to light the fires, but the conflagration did not break forth to sweep the world until the year 1517 when Martin Luther nailed his famous challenge to the Pope on the door of Castle Church in Wittenberg, Germany.

Others advocated reform measures, but it remained for Luther to be *the* Reformer! He used the sledge-hammer that struck the fatal blow against the false paganized system that had come to bear the label of Christianity. The crusade came to a head in the little town of Wittenberg where Luther was teaching in an obscure university.

For several years he had dared to defy the powers at Rome. Different methods had been used to silence him, but without success. He seemed to be entirely without a sense of fear. Being thoroughly nauseated by the secret sins of the priests, the paganism of the Church, the departure from New Testament teachings, and the idea that sins could be remitted by good works, he lost himself in the great consuming ideals of the new reform movement.

Pope Leo was sorely in need of funds with which to rebuild St. Peter's Cathedral at Rome and decided to lift the burden by selling indulgences. A man by the name of John Tetzel, a bold blatant individual, was sent to that part of Germany which included Wittenberg. He was a Dominican monk.

To the crowds who came to hear him speak in the local Castle Church, he exclaimed, "Drop your money in this holy receptacle! Pay for all your sins, past present and future! Help the souls of your deceased relatives that are now in purgatory! *Sobald das Geld im Kasten klingt, die Seele aus dem Fegefeuer in den Himmel springt.* (As soon as the money rattles in the chest, the soul flies from Purgatory into Heaven.)"

This was too much for the pious Luther. God had revealed great light to his soul concerning the fundamental doctrine of grace. He had learned that "THE JUST SHALL LIVE BY FAITH". He saw clearly the Scriptural discrimination between human works and divine grace. Knowing that no amount of self-effort could take the place of the supernatural work of the Holy Spirit in the soul, he resolved to meet the Pope and all his emissaries (including Tetzel), squarely and fight the matter out with this as one of the major issues of the controversy.

The efforts of previous Reformers and the blood of martyred saints who had given their lives in opposing the Roman system was not in vain—because God had raised up a man in the little city of Wittenberg who dared to stand firm in the crisis!

Luther had nothing but contempt for Tetzel and the crass money-raising schemes which he employed. Therefore, on the evening of October 31, 1517 the Augustinian monk walked down the narrow streets of Wittenberg, past the market place and finally reached the imposing structure of the newly built Castle Church.

On this particular night a Hallowe'en celebration was taking place. Farmers and townsmen were on parade, singing folk songs, engaging in pranks and having a merry time in general. Into the excitement walked the serious-minded Luther. His face was stern; he held a piece of paper in one hand and a hammer in the other.

He walked straight to the door of the Church and paused, while hundreds of startled people gazed at him in blank amazement!

"Bang, bang, bang!" With his hammer he nailed his famous document on the door and walked away with deliberate step. His paper contained 95 brief paragraphs; charges against the Roman Catholic Church.

This was the turning point. Here Christianity divided into two major streams. I shall never forget the thrill that came into my soul as I approached the famous entrance to Castle Church for the first time. Here a spiritual rebirth took place. Here Protestantism was born. Under the firm tutorage of Luther, Castle Church became the first Protestant Church in the history of the world. Today there are approximately twenty thousand Protestants and two thousand Catholics in the little city of Wittenberg.

The original wooden door was burned in the war of 1760 by the soldiers of Frederick the Great. In

1858 Kaiser Wilhelm IV made a gift of the beautiful bronze door which the visitor sees at this historic spot today. On the door, the famous 95 Theses are engraved in the Latin language. Inside of Castle Church are the tombs of Luther and his most intimate co-worker, Melanchthon. Nearby in the Wittenberg town square one sees beautiful monuments erected to the memory of these two soldiers of the cross.

THE THESES

THERE is general agreement among students of Bible prophecy that the fifth Church letter of the book of Revelation, addressed to the Church at Sardis, refers to the Reformation period.

Revelation 3:1-4: "And unto the angel of the church in Sardis write; These things saith he that hath the seven Spirits of God, and the seven stars; I know thy works, that thou hast a name that thou livest, and art dead. Be watchful, and strengthen the things which remain, that are ready to die: for I have not found thy works perfect before God. Remember therefore how thou hast received and heard, and hold fast, and repent. If therefore thou shalt not watch, I will come on thee as a thief, and thou shalt not know what hour I will come upon thee. Thou hast a few names even in Sardis which have not defiled their garments; and they shall walk with me in white: for they are worthy."

Corresponding to the above Scripture, we discover that in the awful apostasy which existed during Reformation times, that the Lord had a faithful remnant of loyal ones who had not "defiled their garments".

But even the Reformers, whose very souls cried out against the outrages, were so far from Pentecost and

Castle Church, Wittenberg, Germany. The first Protestant Church in the history of the world. On the door of this edifice Martin Luther nailed his ninety-five Theses.

so close to the pagan idolatry with which the Church was cursed—the doctrine of Grace and the ministry of the Holy Spirit had been lost for such a long time, that their spiritual vision was clouded and the words "thou hast a name that thou livest, and art dead" were really applicable.

This is not meant as a criticism of these faithful warriors for they were walking in all the light that they possessed. They grew up within the scope of pagan Rome and were naturally influenced by her sins. Under these circumstances,however, a high type of spiritual life was impossible. Spiritual vitality came later, in the fire of evangelism which swept the Church —a manifestation of divine power which could not have come to pass had the Reformers not have broken the shackles which had bound Christianity so long.

A study of the 95 Theses, which were considered so revolutionary at the time they were written, show to what extent Luther himself was under the dominance of Roman theological ideas. They show that he actually subscribed, and took for granted, many of the cardinal principles of Catholicism. With the passing of the years, he of course got further and further away from these pagan notions.

Luther's opening challenge and the complete text of the Theses—the document which turned the Church upside down—are as follows:

*   *   *   *

OUT of love for the truth and from desire to elucidate it, the Reverend Father Martin Luther, Master of Arts and Sacred Theology, and ordinary lecturer therein at Wittenberg, intends to defend the following statements and dispute on them in that place. Therefore he asks that those who cannot be present and dispute with him orally shall do so in their absence by letter. In the name of our Lord Jesus Christ, Amen.

1. Our Lord and Master Jesus Christ, in saying,

"Repent ye, etc.," intended that the whole life of his believers on earth should be a constant penance.

2. And the word "penance" neither can, nor may, be understood as referring to the Sacrament of Penance, that is, to confession and atonement as exercised under the priest's ministry.

3. Nevertheless He does not think of inward penance only: rather is inward penance worthless unless it produces various outward mortifications of the flesh.

4. Therefore mortification continues as long as hatred of oneself continues, that is to say, true inward penance lasts until entrance into the Kingdom of Heaven.

5. The Pope will not, and cannot, remit other punishments than those which he has imposed by his own decree or according to the canons.

6. The Pope can forgive sins only in the sense, that he declares and confirms what may be forgiven of God; or that he doth it in those cases which he hath reserved to himself: be this contemned, the sin remains unremitted.

7. God forgives none his sin without at the same time casting him penitent and humbled before the priest His vicar.

8. The canons concerning penance are imposed only on the living; they ought not by any means, following the same canons, to be imposed on the dying.

9. Therefore, the Holy Spirit, acting in the Pope, does well for us, when the latter in his decrees entirely removes the article of death and extreme necessity.

10. Those priests act unreasonably and ill who reserve for Purgatory the penance imposed on the dying.

11. This abuse of changing canonical penalty into the penalty of Purgatory seems to have arisen when the bishops were asleep.

12. In times of yore, canonical penalties were imposed, not after, but before, absolution, as tests of true repentance and affliction.

13. The dying pay all penalties by their death, and are already dead to the canons, and rightly have exemption from them.

14. Imperfect spiritual health or love in the dying person necessarily brings with it great fear; and the less this love is, the greater the fear it brings.

15. This fear and horror—to say nothing of other things—are sufficient in themselves to produce the punishment of Purgatory, because they approximate to the horror of despair.

16. Hell, Purgatory, and Heaven seem to differ as perfect despair, imperfect despair, and security of salvation differ.

17. It seems as must in Purgatory love in the souls increase, as fear diminishes in them.

against the outrages, were so far from Pentecost and

18. It does not seem to be proved either by arguments or by the Holy Writ that they are outside the state of merit and demerit, or increase of love.

19. This, too, seems not to be proved, that they are all sure and confident of their salvation, though we may be quite sure of it.

20 Therefore the Pope, in speaking of the perfect remission of all punishment, does not mean that all penalties in general be forgiven, but only those imposed by himself.

21. Therefore, those preachers of indulgences err who say that, by the Pope's indulgence, a man may be exempt from all punishments, and be saved.

22. Yea, the Pope remits the souls in Purgatory no penalty which they, according to the canons, would have had to pay in this life.

23. If to anybody complete remissions of all penalties may be granted, it is certain that it is granted

only to those most approaching perfection, that is, to very few.

24. Therefore the multitude is misled by the boastful promise of the paid penalty, whereby no manner of distinction is made.

25. The same power that the Pope has over Purgatory, such has also every bishop in his diocese, and every curate in his parish.

26. The Pope acts most rightly in granting remission to souls, not by the power of the keys—which in Purgatory he does not possess—but by way of intercession.

27. They preach vanity who say that the soul flies out of Purgatory as soon as the money thrown into the chest rattles.

28. What is sure, is, that as soon as the penny rattles in the chest, gain and avarice are on the way of increase; but the intercession of the church depends only on the will of God Himself.

29. And who knows, too, whether all those souls in Purgatory wish to be redeemed, as it is said to have happened with St. Severinus and St. Paschalis.

30. Nobody is sure of having repented sincerely enough; much less can he be sure of having received perfect remission of sins.

31. Seldom even as he who has sincere repentance, is he who really gains indulgence; that is to say, most seldom to be found.

32. On the way to eternal damnation are they and their teachers, who believe that they are sure of their salvation through indulgences.

33. Beware well of those who say, the Pope's pardons are that inestimable gift of God by which man is reconciled to God.

34. For the forgiveness contained in these pardons has reference only to the penalties of sacramental atonement which were appointed by men.

35. He preaches like a heathen who teaches that those who will deliver souls out of Purgatory or buy indulgences do not need repentance and contrition.

36. Every Christian who feels sincere repentance and woe on account of his sins, has perfect remission of pain and guilt even without letters of indulgence.

37. Every true Christian, be he still alive or already dead, partaketh in all benefits of Christ and of the Church given him by God, even without letters of indulgence.

38. Yet is the Pope's absolution and dispensation by no means to be contemned, since it is, as I have said, a declaration of the Divine Absolution.

39. It is exceedingly difficult, even for the most subtile theologists, to praise at the same time before the people the great wealth of indulgence and the truth of utter contrition.

40. True repentance and contrition seek and love punishment; while rich indulgence absolves from it, and causes men to hate it, or at least gives them occasion to do so.

41. The Pope's indulgence ought to be proclaimed with all precaution, lest the people should mistakenly believe it of more value than all other works of charity.

42. Christians should be taught, it is not the Pope's opinion that the buying of indulgence is in any way comparable to works of charity.

43. Christians should be taught, he who gives to the poor, or lends to a needy man, does better than buying indulgence.

44. For, by the exercise of charity, charity increases and man grows better, while by means of indulgence, he does not become better, but only freer from punishment.

45. Christians should be taught, he who sees his neighbour in distress, and, nevertheless, buys indulg-

ence, is not partaking in the Pope's pardons, but in the anger of God.

46. Christians should be taught, unless they are rich enough, it is their duty to keep what is necessary for the use of their households, and by no means to throw it away on indulgences.

47. Christians should be taught, the buying of indulgences is optional and not commanded.

48. Christians should be taught, the Pope, in selling pardons, has more want and more desire of a devout prayer for himself than of the money.

49. Christians should be taught, the Pope's pardons are useful as far as one does not put confidence in them, but on the contrary most dangerous, if through them one loses the fear of God.

50. Christians should be taught, if the Pope knew the ways anu doings of the preachers of indulgences, he would prefer that St. Peter's minster should be burnt to ashes, rather than that it should be built up of the skin, flesh, and bones of his lambs.

51. Christians should be taught, the Pope, as it is his bounden duty to do, is indeed also willing to give of his own money—and should St. Peter's be sold thereto—to those from whom the preachers of indulgences do most extort money.

52. It is a vain and false thing to hope to be saved through indulgences though the commissary—nay, the Pope himself—was to pledge his own soul therefore.

53. Those who, on account of a sermon concerning indulgences in one church, condemn the word of God to silence in the others, are enemies of Christ and of the Pope.

54. Wrong is done to the word of God if one in the same sermon spends as much or more time on indulgences as on the word of the Gospel.

55. The opinion of the Pope cannot be otherwise than this: If an indulgence—which is the lowest thing

—be celebrated with one bell, one procession and ceremonies, then the Gospel—which is the highest thing—must be celebrated with a hundred bells, a hundred processions, and a hundred ceremonies.

56. The treasures of the Church, whence the Pope grants his dispensation, are neither sufficiently named nor known among the community of Christ.

57. It is manifest that they are not temporal treasures, for the latter are not lightly spent, but rather gathered by many of the preachers.

58. Nor are they merits of Christ and of the saints, for these, without the Pope's aid, work always grace to the inner man, cross, death, and hell to the outer man.

59. St. Lawrence called the poor of the community the treasures of the community and of the Church, but he understood the word according to the use in his time.

60. We affirm without pertness that the keys of the Church, bestowed through the merit of Christ, are this treasure.

61. For it is clear that the Pope's power is sufficient for the remission of penalties and forgiveness in the reserved cases.

62. The right and true treasure of the Church is the most Holy Gospel of the glory and grace of God.

63. This treasure, however, is deservedly most hateful, for it makes the first to be the last.

64. While the treasure of indulgence is deservedly most agreeable, for it makes the last to be the first.

65. Therefore, the treasures of the Gospel are nets, with which, in times of yore, one fished for the men of Mammon.

66. But the treasures of indulgence are nets, with which now-a-days one fishes for the Mammon of men.

67. Those indulgences, which the preachers pro-

claim to be great mercies are indeed great mercies, forasmuch as they promote gain.

68. And yet they are of the smallest compared to the grace of God and to the devotion of the Cross.

69. Bishops and curates ought to mark with eyes and ears, that the commissaries of apostolical (that is, Popish) pardons are received with all reverence.

70. But they ought still more to mark with eyes and ears, that these commissaries do not preach their own fancies instead of what the Pope has commanded.

71. He who speaks against the truth of apostolical pardons, be anathema and accursed.

72. But blessed be he who is on his guard against the preacher's of pardons naughty and impudent words.

73. As the Pope justly disgraces and excommunicates those who use any kind of contrivance to do damage to the traffic in indulgences,

74. Much more it is his intention to disgrace and excommunicate those who, under the pretext of indulgences, use contrivance to do damage to holy love and truth.

75. To think that the Popish pardons have power to absolve a man even if—to utter an impossibility—he had violated the Mother of God, is madness.

76. We assert on the contrary that the Popish pardons cannot take away the least of daily sins, as regards the guilt of it.

77. To say that St. Peter, if he were now Pope, could show no greater mercies, is blasphemy against St. Peter and the Pope.

78. We assert on the contrary that both this and every other Pope has greater mercies to show: namely, the Gospel, spiritual powers, gifts of healing, etc. (1. Cor. XII).

79. He who says that the cross with the Pope's

arms, solemnly set on high, has as much power as the Cross of Christ, blasphemes God.

80. Those bishops, curates, and theologists, who allow such speeches to be uttered among the people, will have one day to answer for it.

81. Such impudent sermons concerning indulgences make it difficult even for learned men to protect the Pope's honour and dignity against the calumnies, or at all events against the searching questions, of the laymen.

82. As for instance:—Why does not the Pope deliver all souls at the same time out of Purgatory for the sake of most holy love and on account of the bitterest distress of those souls—this being the most imperative of all motives,—while he saves an infinite number of souls for the sake of that most miserable thing money, to be spent on St. Peter's minster—this be withdrawn the funds which were established for the sake of the dead, since it is now wrong to pray for those who are already saved?

84. Again:—What is this new holiness of God and the Pope that, for money's sake, they permit the wicked and the enemy of God to save a pious soul, faithful to God, and yet will not save that pious and beloved soul without payment, out of love, and on account of its great distress?

85. Again:—Why is it that the canons of penance, long abrogated and dead in themselves, because they are not used, are yet still paid for with money through the granting of pardons, as if they were still in force and alive?

86. Again:—Why does not the Pope build St. Peter's Minster with his own money—since his riches being the very slightest of motives?

83. Or again:—Why do masses for the dead continue, and why does not the Pope return or permit to

are now more ample than those of Crassus,—rather
than with money of poor Christians?

87. Again:—Why does the Pope remit or give to
those who, through perfect penitence, have already a
right to plenary remission and pardon?

88. Again:—What greater good could the Church
receive, than if the Pope presented this remission and
pardon a hundred times a day to every believer, instead
of but once, as he does now?

89. If the Pope seeks by his pardons the salvation
of souls, rather than money, why does he annul letters
of indulgence granted long ago, and declare them out
of force, though they are still in force?

90. To repress these very telling questions of the
layman only by force, and not to solve them by telling
the truth, is to expose the Church and the Pope to
the enemy's ridicule and to make Christian people un-
happy.

91. Therefore, if pardons were preached according
to the Pope's intention and opinion, all these objections
would be easily answered, nay, they never had occur-
red.

92. Away then with all those prophets who say to
the community of Christ, "Peace, peace," and there is
no peace.

93. But blessed be all those prophets who say to
the community of Christ, "The cross, the cross," and
there is no cross.

94. Christians should be exhorted to endeavour to
follow Christ their Head through Cross, Death, and
Hell,

95. And thus hope with confidence to enter Heaven
through many miseries, rather than in false security.

THE REFORMATION

NATURALLY Luther's opposition interfered with the Church's financial returns from the sale of indulgences. This was the thing that seemed to cause Rome the most grief.

It was the Pope's usual policy to ignore opposition and thus destroy it with indifference. But Luther's bombardment was too well timed and his engines of warfare were too powerful to be passed over lightly. The insolent young professor was therefore summoned to come to Rome.

At this point, Luther's friend Frederick the Wise, who governed Saxony in which Wittenberg was located, interfered because he was afraid for the Reformer's welfare. Thereupon the Pope consented to grant Luther a hearing at home. The city of Augsburg was selected and a Dominican monk named Cajetan was selected to serve as judge.

Cajetan showed utmost contempt for the Reformer but this did not seem to bother Luther in the least. The report sent to Rome following the Augsburg trial contained nothing in Luther's favor.

Meanwhile, hundreds of new converts were being made every week to the cause of the Reformation.

The Church blundered again when a theologian by the name of Eck was selected to debate Luther on the subject of indulgences. Eck made a poor showing. During one of his arguments Luther said, "I recognize the authority of the Bible only." Until this time he had not disputed the authority of the Church in spiritual matters. This attitude was regarded as rank heresy.

It was June 15, 1520 that the Pope sent a document—a Papal bull—to the young professor giving him two months in which to recant or suffer excommunication. The bull contained forty-one charges against Luther and his teachings.

This was a dramatic hour in the history of the Reformation. Instead of cringing like a weakling, Luther shook his fist in the Pope's face, took the papers he had received from Rome to a spot under a nearby oak tree and started a bonfire with them. He was followed and cheered by a large crowd including many of his students in Wittenberg University.

When the Pope's bull of excommunication was received later, Luther showed only scorn for its contents. No wonder people were willing to follow such a courageous leader!

Philip Melanchthon, a fellow professor, stood firm on the side of the Reformation throughout the entire struggle. The two men worked together in perfect harmony.

The fatal day came when Luther was instructed to appear before the imperial Diet in the city of Worms. Friends begged him not to go but he gave his famous answer, "I am determined to enter Worms although as many devils set on me, as there are tiles on the housetops."

His flaming eloquence, logic, voice of thunder, his withering sarcasm, delivered before the assembly of officials and Churchmen, is one of the most significant scenes of history. When ordered definitely to recant, he replied, "Unless I am convinced by Scripture and reason, I neither can, nor dare retract anything; for my conscience is a captive to the Word of God, and it is neither safe nor right to go against conscience. There I take my stand. I can do no otherwise. So help me God. Amen."

The Diet sentenced him an outlaw. Being placed in this position any one could kill him without being afraid of suffering arrest for the crime. On his way back to Wittenberg, Frederick the Wise had him kidnapped and held in a secret place for ten months during which time he started his translation of the New Testament into the German language.

This was the man, the battering-ram God used, to open the clogged channels so that the water from the Rock of Pentecost could continue to flow through the centuries.